LifeCycles

Egg to Chicken

Camilla de la Bédoyère

QEB Publishing

Copyright © QEB Publishing, Inc. 2009

This edition published by Scholastic Inc., 557 Broadway,
New York, NY 10012, by arrangement with
QEB Publishing, Inc., 3 Wrigley, Suite A, Irvine, CA 92618

www.qeb-publishing.com

Library of Congress Cataloging-in-Publication Data

De la Bédoyère, Camilla.
  Egg to chicken / Camilla de la Bedoyere.
      p. cm. -- (QEB life cycles)
  Includes index.
  ISBN 978-1-59566-741-0 (hardcover)
  1. Chickens--Life cycles--Juvenile literature. I. Title.
  SF487.5.D45 2010
  636.5--dc22

                                        2009000391

Printed and bound in China

ISBN: 978 0 545 22483 3 (paperback)

10 9 8 7 6 5 4 3 2 1

Author Camilla de la Bédoyère
Editor Angela Royston
Designer and Picture Researcher Melissa Alaverdy

Publisher Steve Evans
Creative Director Zeta Davies
Managing Editor Amanda Askew

Words in **bold** are explained in the glossary on page 22.

Picture credits
(t=top, b=bottom, l=left, r=right, c=center, fc=front cover)
Corbis 1t Holger Winkler/AB/zefa, 1b Craig Holmes/Loop Images, 5t Martin
Harvey, 6–7 Craig Holmes/Loop Images, 11b Holger Winkler/AB/zefa
Getty Images 10–11 Georgette Douwma, 11t Bob Elsdale, 12 Dorling
Kindersley, 15b Tara Moore, 17t Jane Burton, 17b GK Hart/
Vikki Hart, 18 Klaus Nigge
Photolibrary Group 9t John Cancalosi, 13 Harald Lange, 14 Andre
Maslennikov, 20–21 Harald Lange
Shutterstock 2t iofoto, 4b Dee Hunter, 4–5 Valio, 5b JanJar, 6b JanJar,
6t Gelpi, 8 Craig Hanson, 8 Craig Hanson, 9b Babusi Octavian Florentin,
15t AGphotographer, 16b Saied Shahin Kiya, 16c Saied Shahin Kiya, 16t Saied
Shahin Kiya, 19 Babusi Octavian Florentin, 20l Jozsef Szasz-Fabian,
22–23 Vasyl Helevachuk, 24 Saied Shahin Kiya

Contents

What is a Chicken?

A chicken is a type of bird. All birds have feathers and wings, and lay eggs.

Feathers help birds fly, and stay warm and dry. Flying takes a lot of energy, so birds need to eat often.

⇩Birds have mouths called beaks or bills, but no teeth.

⇧ Gulls spread their wings and feathery tails when they fly.

Most birds build **nests** to lay eggs and keep their young safe and sheltered. Domestic chickens build their nests in boxes.

Ostrich egg

⇨One ostrich egg weighs the same as 24 hen eggs.

⇧Ostriches have wings, but cannot fly. Ostriches are the world's largest birds.

Hen egg

The Story of a Chicken

There are more chickens in the world than any other type of bird.

A hen is a female chicken. A male chicken is called a rooster. A chick is a baby chicken.

Chicks begin their lives as eggs. The story of how an egg grows into an adult chicken is called a **life cycle**.

⇨ A chicken goes through three stages in its life cycle.

2

Chick

1

Egg

Making a Nest

Hens start laying eggs when they are around six months old. First, they need a **nest** to lay the eggs in.

Most birds build their nests in trees. They may use twigs, grass, or moss.

⇐ Ospreys build huge nests of twigs in trees and on rooftops.

⇨ The smallest nests are built by hummingbirds.

Hens build their nests on the ground. They find somewhere dry and quiet, and use straw or grass to make the nest.

⇩ Hens build their nests in barns or hen houses, where they are warm and safe.

The Eggs are Laid

A hen usually lays one egg a day. These eggs will be **fertilized** and grow into chicks if a rooster is living with the hen.

Roosters are bigger than hens, and they can crow loudly. Hens make a quieter, clucking sound.

⇦ A rooster also crows to tell other males to stay away.

⇨ Roosters have longer tail feathers than hens.

⇨ Hens can lay eggs every day.

The hen normally lays several eggs in her nest. A group of eggs is called a **clutch**.

Brooding

When the hen has laid all her eggs in the nest, she sits on them to keep them warm. This is called **brooding**, and it is an important job.

The hen has to sit on her clutch. If the eggs become cold, the chicks inside stop growing.

⇨ A brooding hen spreads her feathers over the eggs.

⇧ A nesting box makes a safe, warm home for hens and their eggs.

The hen turns the eggs from time to time to keep them warm all-over.

Inside the Egg

All bird eggs are protected by a hard **shell**. Inside each fertilized egg, a tiny chick is growing.

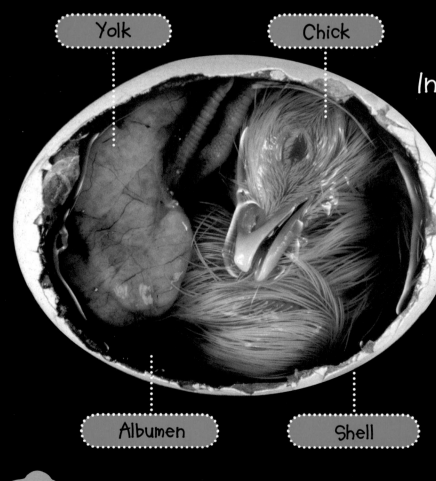

Yolk

Chick

Albumen

Shell

Inside the egg, the chick gets food from the yellow **yolk** and **albumen**. The albumen is the clear liquid that we call the white of the egg. It protects the chick and keeps it warm.

⇦ Chicks need air to breathe. The larger end of the egg holds an air space.

The eggs we eat have not been fertilized. They do not have chicks inside them.

⇧ Most chicken egg shells are brown, white, or cream.

⇨ Chicken eggs are easy to cook and good to eat!

The Eggs Hatch

After growing for about three weeks, the young chicks are ready to break out of their eggs. This is called **hatching**.

Each chick has a sharp point on their top beak, called an egg-tooth.

3

⇧ It uses its body to push the shell apart.

2

⇦ It chips a hole all around the shell.

1

⇦ The chick uses its egg-tooth to crack a hole in the shell.

4 ⇐ Then it climbs out of the shell.

The newly hatched chick cheeps loudly. It is tired and its feathers are wet. Once the feathers have dried, they become fluffy.

5

⇒ Soon all the chicks have hatched.

Life as a Chick

The hen looks after her newly hatched chicks. She keeps them warm under her wings.

When they are just two weeks old, the chicks can leave the barn or hen house and explore outside.

⇦ Newly hatched chicks stay close to their mother.

Chicks and chickens like to scratch around in the dirt, looking for tasty worms or bugs to eat.

⇨Chickens do not have teeth, so they cannot chew their food. They swallow it whole.

Growing and Changing

Chicks grow into adults in just a few months. Glossy feathers grow in place of the soft, fluffy feathers.

The chicks grow red, fleshy combs on top of their heads. The combs help keep them cool.

⇧ A hen that is less than one year old is called a pullet.

Soon the young hens will start to lay eggs. When a hen mates, a new life cycle begins.

⇩Roosters have colorful feathers and grow larger combs than hens.

Rooster comb

Glossary

Albumen
The white of an egg.

Brooding
When a hen sits on her eggs to keep them warm.

Clutch
A group of eggs.

Comb
The soft, red skin on top of a chicken's head.

Fertilize
When a special cell from a male joins with a female's egg to form a new living thing.

Hatching
When a chick breaks out of its egg.

Life cycle
The story of how an animal changes from birth to death, and how it produces young.

Nest
A safe place that birds make so they can lay their eggs.

Pullet
A chick that is less than one year old.

Shell
The hard outside of an egg. It protects the chick inside.

Yolk
The yellow part of an egg. The yolk is food for the chick inside

Index

Notes for parents and teachers

 Picture this
Look through the book and talk about the pictures. Read the captions and ask questions about other things in the photographs that have not been mentioned in the text.

 Respect for wildlife
Find out more about birds by watching them in the wild. Help children use a guidebook to identify different birds. Remind them that nests and eggs should never be approached or disturbed.

 Science at home
Carry out some simple experiments with an egg. Try rolling it on a smooth surface and watch how it moves. See what happens when you float an egg in water (the freshest eggs sink).

Open the egg and identify the parts. Hard boil an egg and talk about the way heat changes the contents.

 Family tree
Talking about a child's family helps them to link life processes to their own experience. Drawing simple family trees, looking at photos, and talking to grandparents are fun ways to engage young children.

QEB Publishing

Tadpole to Frog

Camilla de la Bédoyère

Copyright © QEB Publishing, Inc. 2009

This edition published by Scholastic Inc., 557 Broadway,
New York, NY 10012, by arrangement with
QEB Publishing, Inc., 3 Wrigley, Suite A, Irvine, CA 92618

www.qeb-publishing.com

Scholastic and associated logos are trademarks and/or registered
trademarks of Scholastic Inc.
Distributed by Scholastic Canada Ltd; Markham, Ontario

Library of Congress Cataloging-in-Publication Data

De la Bédoyère, Camilla.
  Tadpole to frog / Camilla de la Bédoyère.
    p. cm. -- (QEB life cycles)
  Includes bibliographical references and index.
  ISBN 978-1-59566-738-0 (hardcover)
  1. Frogs--Lifecycles--Juvenile literature. 2. Tadpoles--Juvenile
literature. I. Title.
  QL668.E2D394 2010
  597.8'9156--dc22

                                            2009001118

Printed and bound in China

ISBN: 978 0 545 22483 3 (paperback)

10 9 8 7 6 5 4 3 2 1

Author Camilla de la Bédoyère
Editor Angela Royston
Designer and Picture Researcher Melissa Alaverdy

Publisher Steve Evans
Creative Director Zeta Davies
Managing Editor Amanda Askew

Words in **bold**
are explained in
the glossary on
page 22.

Picture credits
(t=top, b=bottom, l=left, r=right, c=center, fc=front cover)
Corbis 6t Martin B Withers/Frank Lane Picture Agency
FLPA 4 Malcolm Schuyl, 8–9 Derek Middleton, 10–11 Wil
Meinderts/FN/Minden, 15 Jef Meul/FN/Minden, 19b Fritz Polking,
20t Roger Tidman
Getty Images 18–19 Frank Greenaway, 20–21 Christoph Burki
naturepl.com 12–13 Jane Burton
NHPA 14l George Bernard, 14c George Bernard, 14t George
Bernard, 16–17 Stephen Dalton, 17r T Kitchin & V Hurst,
24b George Bernard
Photolibrary Group 1t Oxford Scientific, 1b Elliott Neep,
6–7 Elliott Neep, 21t Markus Botzek
Shutterstock 2t Knorre, 3 jgl247, 5r Sebastian Duda, 5r Fizpok,
5l Ismael Montero Verdu, 5t Sebastian Duda, 7t Thomas Mounsey,
23 Sebastian Duda, 23t Ismael Montero Verdu, 23r Sebastian Duda

Contents

What is a Frog?

A frog is an **amphibian**. It spends
part of its life living in water,
and part of its life on land.

Amphibians lay their eggs in water.
They live in wet places, often
near ponds or lakes.

⇦ Common frogs
have smooth,
damp skin and
golden eyes.

Foot

Eye

⇨ This tree frog's big, red eyes and orange feet scare other animals away.

Some frogs live in wet rain forests. They are called tree frogs. Most tree frogs are much smaller than frogs that live on the ground.

The Story of a Frog

Frogs begin life as an egg. The amazing story of how they become adult frogs is called a life cycle.

A young frog is called a **tadpole**. It looks different from a frog!

Egg

1

1

Frog

3

⇨ A frog goes through three stages in its life cycle. The first two stages are spent in water.

Tadpole

2

Frogspawn

A female frog lays her eggs in spring. She always lays them in water.

She lays hundreds of eggs where the water is shallow. The eggs float on the water's surface.

⇨ The frogspawn swells
and floats to the
surface of the water.

Frog eggs are soft and squishy.
They stick together in a big
clump called **frogspawn**.

⇦ A female frog
may lay hundreds
of eggs at a time.

Inside the Eggs

Once the eggs are laid, the adult frogs swim away. Inside each egg, a new tadpole is growing.

The tadpole feeds on a small **yolk** in the egg, and grows bigger.

Many eggs are eaten by fish and other pond animals. But some survive, and their tadpoles keep growing.

After a few weeks, the eggs hatch. They hatch sooner in warm weather than they do in cold weather.

Tiny Tadpoles

Tadpoles are tiny when they hatch, but they quickly grow.

Each tadpole has a long tail, which it uses to swim. It has feathery **gills** on either side of its head. These allow the young tadpole to breathe underwater.

To begin with, tadpoles just eat small, green water plants. Later, they will also eat pond animals, such as water fleas.

⇨Tadpoles grow faster when they live in warm water with plenty of food.

Tail

12

Gills

The Big Change

When they are about seven weeks old, tadpoles begin to change into frogs.

First, they grow back legs. A few weeks later, their gills disappear. Then they swim to the surface of the water to breathe air.

3

⇧ As its legs grow longer, the tail grows shorter.

2

1

⇦ Then its front legs begin to grow.

⇦ The tadpole's back legs grow first.

14

Frogs' tails begin to shrink and their front legs begin to grow. The tadpoles now look like tiny frogs.

4

⇩By the time it is 12 weeks old, the tiny frog is about 1 inch (3 centimeters) long.

Froglets

The little frogs keep growing, and their tails disappear. They are now called froglets.

The froglets stay in, or near, water. They feed on small **insects**, which they catch with their long, sticky tongues.

⇨ Froglets can swim, crawl, hop, and climb onto the floating leaves of lilies.

When they are bigger,
the froglets move away
from their pond.

They find a safe
place under plants,
where they hide.

⇨ This froglet
is hiding in a
pitcher plant.

The Life of a Frog

Adult frogs spend most of their time on land. They hide from animals that hunt them.

Frogs rest during the day. In the evening, they hunt for insects, slugs, and worms.

⇩Frogs can make huge leaps to catch food with their long tongues.

Tongue

⇩Camouflage helps a frog to hide from animals that want to eat it.

Many frogs have green, gray, or brown skin. They blend in with their surroundings and are hard to see. This is called **camouflage**.

Back to the Pond

Frogs **hibernate** in winter.
This is because there is
little food to eat and
the weather is cold.

When animals hibernate,
they fall into a deep
sleep to save energy.

⇧ Frogs hibernate under
rocks, in burrows, or
in ponds.

In spring, frogs return to the pond where they were born. Soon the story of the life cycle will begin again.

⇩Male tree frogs croak loudly to call the female.

⇩Frogs are ready to mate when they are two to three years old.

21

Glossary

Amphibian
An animal that spends the first part of its life cycle in water, and the second part mostly on land.

Camouflage
Patterns and colors that help an animal hide.

Fertilize
When liquid from a male changes female eggs so that they can grow into new living things.

Frogspawn
A clump of frog's eggs.

Gills
The parts of a tadpole's body that allow it to breathe underwater.

Hibernate
To spend the cold winter months in a kind of deep sleep.

Insect
A small animal with six legs. A water flea is a type of insect.

Life cycle
The story of how a living thing changes from birth to death and how it has young.

Rain forest
A forest that has a lot of rain all year round.

Tadpole
A young frog that hatches from its egg and spends all the time in water.

Yolk
The part of an egg that feeds the growing tadpole.

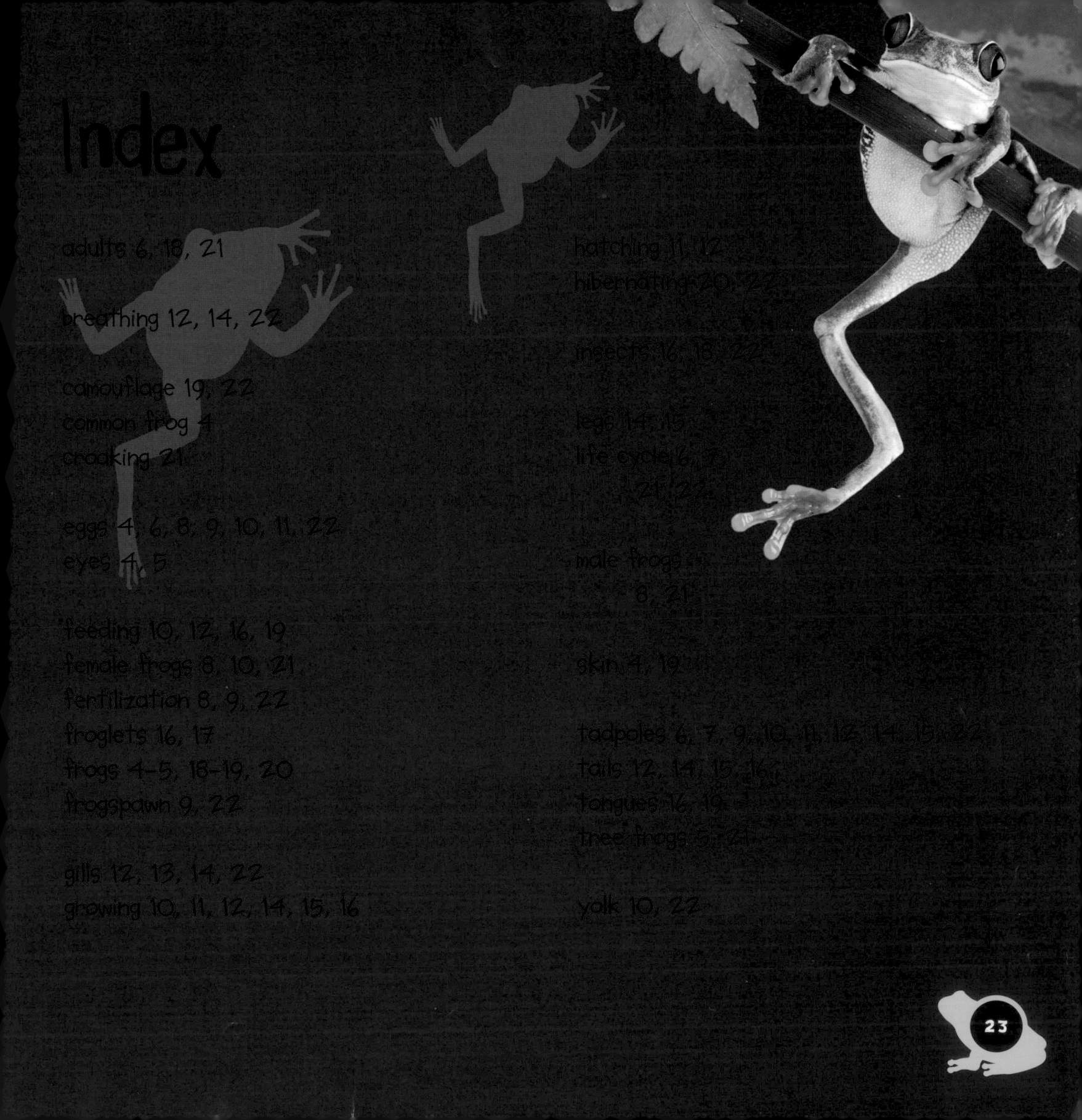

Index

Notes for Parents and Teachers

 Safety outdoors
Teach children how to stay safe while investigating animals and their life cycles, especially when they are around water.

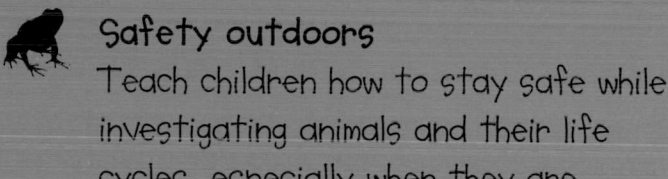 **Respect for wildlife**
Teach children how to observe and, if appropriate, handle animals with care. They should observe animals in their natural environment, without disturbing wildlife and their habitats. Frogspawn should not be moved from one pond to another, as this could spread viruses and other diseases.

 **Frog activities**
Draw the life cycle of a frog and label the different stages together. Use the Internet to research different kinds of frogs and find out more about them.

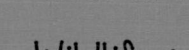 **Wildlife park**
Visit a wildlife park together to learn about pond habitats. Talk about the ways that a habitat provides an animal with the food and shelter it needs to survive. Find out about the other animals that live in a pond habitat.

 Family tree
Talking about a child's family helps them to link life processes to their own experience. Drawing simple family trees and looking at photo albums are fun ways to engage children.